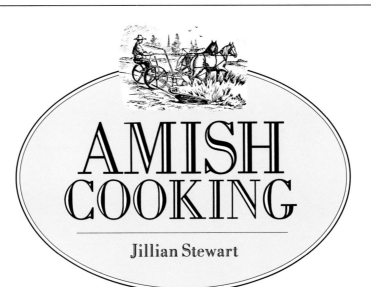

AMISH
COOKING

Jillian Stewart

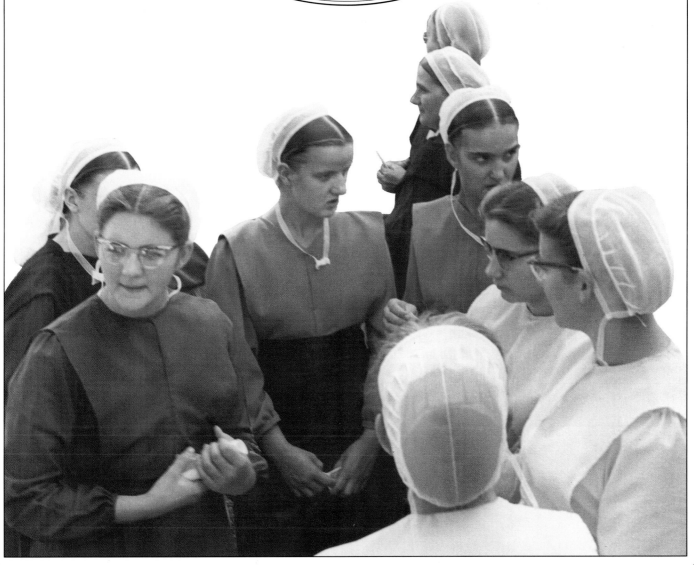

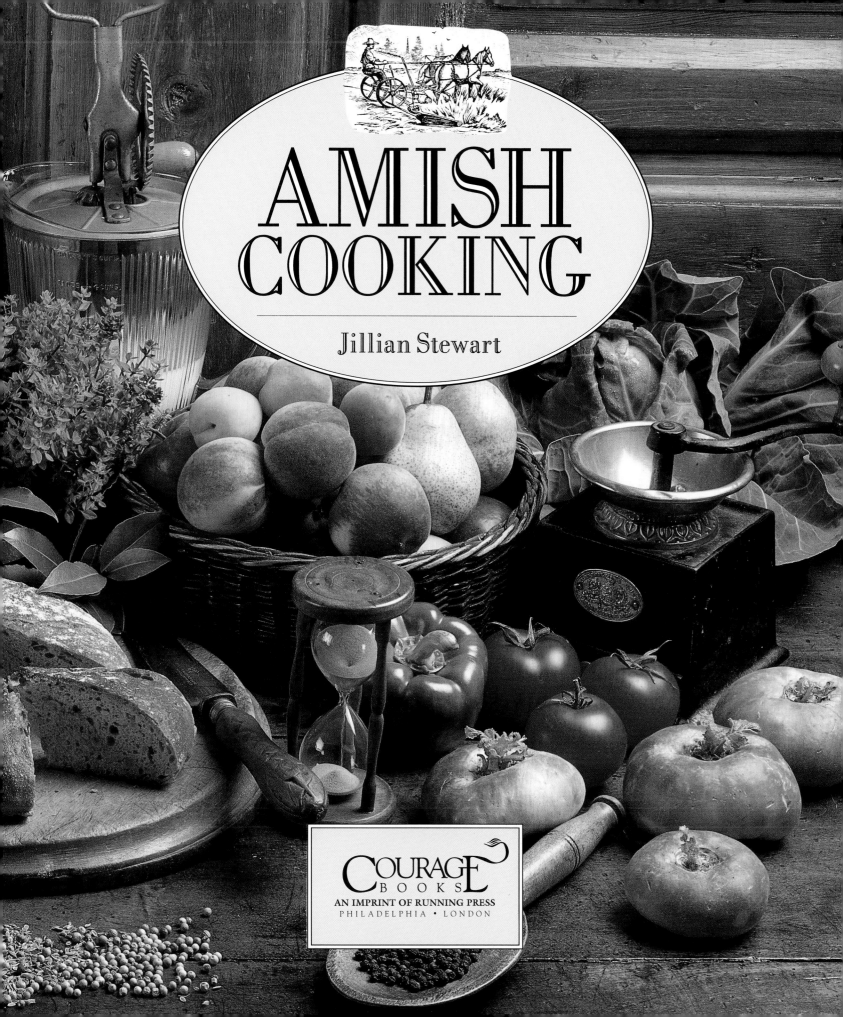

AMISH COOKING

Jillian Stewart

COURAGE
BOOKS

AN IMPRINT OF RUNNING PRESS
PHILADELPHIA · LONDON

CLB 4275
9 8 7 6 5 4 3 2 1
Digit on the right indicates the number of this
printing.

Library of Congress Cataloging-in-Publication
Number 94-72597

ISBN 1-56138-562-X

This book was designed and produced by
CLB Publishing, Godalming, Surrey, England.

Editor: Jillian Stewart
Introduction: Bill Harris
Designer: Alison Lee
Picture Researcher: Leora Kahn
Food Photography: Neil Sutherland and
    Peter Barry
Amish Photography: Copyright © 1960 - Mel Horst

Typesetting by Dorwyn
Printed and bound in Singapore

Published by Courage Books,
an imprint of Running Press Book Publishers
125 South Twenty-second Street
Philadelphia, PA 19103-4399

*Right: the tranquility of an Amish farm
belies the constant hard work and care
needed to run a farm with out the
convenience of modern machinery.*

Contents

Introduction

Above: the kitchen remains at the heart of life on an Amish farm. Although some Amish use kerosene and gas stoves, most still cook on wood burning stoves.

In Pennsylvania, Ohio, Indiana and any of the hundreds of other areas in the United States and Canada where the Amish and other Plain People have settled down, they have become something of a tourist attraction. In general, they don't mind the attention, as long as it doesn't get in the way of the work that has to be done, and they are usually patient with outsiders they think of as either "English," or "city people." Patience, after all, is one of the virtues that rules their lives. But if the outsiders find them a bit odd, the feeling is quite mutual. One of them sums up the difference by saying, ". . . In the city you never know where your wife is, and city women can't cook."

Some city people might take exception to that, but for all of us, Amish or not, the capacity to enjoy hearty

Right: a typical Amish farm.

7

country cooking is basic to our American heritage. The Amish celebrate their German and Swiss roots in theirs, but many of the recipes in the following pages might have been handed down by your own grandmother, even though her own roots may have been in England or Ireland, Russia or Poland, because in nineteenth-century America, just about everybody enjoyed similar fare. The vast majority of our ancestors lived in farm communities and such food was as all-American as, well, apple pie.

The pies often come from a supermarket freezer these days, bread dough is kneaded with a hook attached to heavy-duty electric mixer, soups are run through a food processor and many cooks who take great pride in their work couldn't make a batch of doughnuts without a thermostat-controlled frying pan. There is nothing wrong with modern conveniences, of course, but the good news is that the nineteenth century is still alive and well in Amish kitchens where neither the words "modern" nor "convenience" are ever heard and, as you'll see for yourself, it can easily be brought to life in your own.

Especially in east-central Pennsylvania, where the term "Amish Country" has crept into tourist brochures, not all of America's Plain People call themselves Amish. But all of them have made important contributions to keeping the old style of cooking part of our heritage, even though it, too, is most often called Amish cooking.

It all began during the Protestant Reformation. After Martin Luther called for reform in the old medieval Church, Europe's common people took it as an opportunity to reform society itself. In time, it became apparent to many of them that it would be an impossible

Above: the Mennonite Church at Paradise, Pennsylvania.

task and some did the next best thing by withdrawing into closed communities of their own. Most of the new beliefs were sincere attempts to refine Luther's teachings, but some rejected him completely for what they considered his papist leanings. Among them was a group that called themselves Anabaptists, a distinctly new religion that was formed in Holland in 1525.

Over the years, the Anabaptists began disagreeing among themselves and broke up into smaller groups, including one that still exists, the Mennonites, who rallied around the teachings of the Dutch reformer Menno Simons. Central to all Anabaptist belief is that baptism should not be administered to babies, but to adults in the tradition of John the Baptist. Beyond that, they base their faith on a strict interpretation of the Sermon on the Mount, and renouncing all the evils of the world from participation in wars and politics to incurring debt. In the case of the Mennonites, Simons went a bit further in stressing a complete break with the world with the adoption of plain speech, plain dress and plain lifestyles, but although none of his followers objected to following those rules, there were still some among them who thought he didn't go nearly far enough with the rest of them.

Among the dissidents was Jakob Ammann, a Mennonite minister who broke with Simons and his disciples in the 1690s over the church's practice of Meidung, which in more recent times has come to be called "shunning." The idea was that any member of the Mennonite Church who was excommunicated would be avoided by all the other members until reinstated through confession and true repentance. When a woman was excommunicated for lying, the community became divided over whether the punishment fitted the crime, and when church leaders seemed ready to forgive her, Ammann was incensed and bolted from the fold taking his congregation with him. He toured other Mennonite congregations in Alsace and Switzerland demanding stricter rules, along with an end to what he considered creeping liberalism.

Those ministers who didn't agree with him were excommunicated in Ammann's opinion and it followed that since his coreligionists were thus subject to shunning, he had no choice but to form a religion of his own, which came to be known as Amish in honor of its founder. It followed the same rules that bound the Mennonites together, but strengthened most of them, particularly Meidung. According to Ammann, shunning was a universal rule that even extended to marriage partners who must avoid their excommunicated spouses even to the extent of forbidding them to eat at the same table with faithful family members. As far as the Mennonites were concerned, shunning was a spiritual thing and did not necessarily extend into one's daily secular life.

The rebel minister also added a long list of new restrictions to the established dress code, insisting on much more plainness than Simons had proscribed, and insituted a new rule that men were forbidden to trim their beards. Nearly all of his rules have been modified over the years, though none has been repealed. In our time, Amish men do trim their beards when they're young and they don't allow them grow out until they have been married, at which time the whiskers become the Amish equivalent of a wedding ring. They also carefully shave their upper lip because nineteenth-century soldiers sported moustaches as a badge of honor and the Amish, who refuse to serve in any man's army, began removing theirs as a defiant reversal of the symbolism.

Once the split was formalized, the Amish moved across the border from Switzerland to Alsace and from there persecution forced them deeper into France and Germany until the Napoleonic Wars drove them to North America. By the first quarter of the nineteenth century, there were no Amish left anywhere in Europe.

They found a better life in America where there was land in abundance and for the first time they were able to establish communities of their own. They had lived on scattered farms in Europe, and in many places, the family itself constituted a congregation. Services were held in their homes, and twice a year they trekked great distances to other Amish farms for the required communion services. Their scattered existence also presented them with another problem because marriage with outsiders was strictly forbidden. It was a problem compounded by the fact that the Amish never looked for converts, but expected their religon to continue through their children. In America, all that changed. Not only did they have close contact with like-minded people, but there was far less prejudice to overcome.

Although they eventually migrated to other parts of America, the earliest destination of emigrating Amish was Pennsylvania. In establishing his colony, William Penn had followed a plan to provide a haven for his fellow Quakers and for other persecuted religions of the world. He was especially interested in the Mennonites of the German Palatine whose farming skills and steady habits he believed would help the colony thrive. He offered them land at ten cents an acre and they began arriving in 1688, five years before the split that created the Amish.

All the Plain People there are still called "Pennsylvania Dutch," from their German language, "Deutsch," and the majority of them are Mennonites, even though they are said to live in "Amish Country." But they are far from the only two groups. Among their neighbors are Schwenkfelders, whose beliefs go back to Kaspar Schwenkfeld von Ossig, a Silesian nobleman who thought that Martin Luther's ideas were much too conservative, with the result that Luther himself denounced him as a heretic, earning him the animosity of both Catholics and Protestants. His followers were essentially Anabaptists, and when they began arriving in Pennsylvania in 1743, they were welcomed by Mennonites and Quakers alike because both groups recognized themselves in Schwenkfelder belief.

Almost a generation earlier, the entire population of another Anabaptist sect, the Church of the Brethren, pulled up stakes in Germany and resettled in Pennsylvania. They celebrated their arrival with a Christmas Day baptismal ceremony in the icy waters of a creek near Germantown, an occasion that earned them the name "Dunkers," which they have been called ever since. Their baptismal beliefs, as well as their dress codes are quite similar to the Mennonites, but they believe that no one can be truly baptized until plunged face-first into the icy waters of a fast-moving stream.

Among the other religions that joined the Pennsylvania melting pot was the Moravians, whose Protestant roots go back to the teachings of Jan Hus, who was burned at the stake for his antichurch heresies a century before the Reformation. Most of the migrating Moravians had been artistocrats in what is now the Czech Republic, and the communes they established in Pennsylvania stressed culture and fine art, quite the opposite of the teachings of the Anabaptists. But they shared the concept of living apart, and in spite of their differences, outsiders today usually consider Moravians to be representative of the Plain People.

What all of the Plain People have in common is the joy of family life, and it reaches its height in their kitchens where the job of feeding the family is close to a religious experience in itself. It is a joy that is frequently shared with other families, too, most notably in the form of wedding feasts.

The big events are restaged time after time in Amishland in November and December, a season dictated by the rhythms of farm life. The harvest is in, giving families a focus on their financial condition; and the butchering is done, freeing them to enjoy the kind of socializing weddings bring. An early winter wedding also allows the bride and groom a chance to begin their new life at a time when there is less work to be done on the farm and there is time to get to know one another better. Amish weddings never take place during a waning moon, and never in a leap year, and invariably they are held on a Tuesday or a Thursday. Although the day is chosen for some practical reasons, old superstitions also enter in. A Sunday wedding would be unthinkable because it is a day of rest. Because of that, it would also be unthinkable to schedule a wedding on a Monday because of the preparation required the day before. Wednesday is often called the Devil's Day, reflecting an old Christian tradition that it became a day of infamy the night Judas Iscariot betrayed Jesus Christ, and the Amish are still reluctant to bring any hint of betrayal into a wedding celebration. Friday, the day Christ suffered on the Cross, is also considered a poor choice. Indeed, the Amish strongly believe that anything at all begun on a Friday, from the planting of crops to the butchering of cattle, will come to a bad end. Finally, Saturday is out of the question because it is a day of preparation for the Sabbath, and it would be unseemly to have a house disheveled on the Lord's Day. Of the two choices left, Tuesday is a lucky day, especially because folk wisdom holds that the power of witches is at its lowest ebb on the third day of the week. But Thursday is the most popular choice because it has the advantage of being far enough from the Sabbath to allow time to put together a perfect feast. Anything less would be a discredit to the bride.

On the day before an Amish wedding, two young men, designated by the bridegroom as his witnesses, arrive at the bride's home, where the groom himself has been living since their engagement was announced. Their job is to help with the heavy work of setting up tables and any other last-minute chores, but they are not the only guests in the house. Two bridesmaids are also there to help in the kitchen. All four will remain until the day after the wedding, when they will be in charge of cleaning up.

The bride's parents, who do no work on the wedding day, have previously sent special invitations to family and friends giving them the honor of cooking and serving the food, which for an average Amish wedding means preparing two full meals for two or three hundred guests. The first and most important of the feasts must be ready the moment the first guests begin arriving from the wedding, which has taken place in another home. Since the ceremony typically lasts two or three hours, it is certain they will arrive hungry.

The traditional meal that welcomes them includes a meat course, usually chicken, but sometimes veal, symbolizing the biblical fatted calf, along with a stuffing and mashed potatoes, usually served with homemade sausage. The well-laden table will also include a wide variety of cold meats, along with celery and carrots, several different kinds of cheeses, pickles, canned fruit and piles of cookies as well as huge loaves of freshly made bread served with both creamery butter and apple butter. Angel food cake is the dessert of choice, but there are plenty of pies, too, as well as apple strudel and cheesecake. Needless to say, except for the celery and carrots, which come directly from Amish kitchen gardens, all of it is homemade.

It is a leisurely meal, intended to last most of the afternoon, and everyone is encouraged to keep refilling their plates from platters and bowls that themselves are kept filled through the entire feast. Dinner music is provided by the church choir, and the guests join them in the hymn-singing between courses. Even after the meal has ended, the cold items are left in place for the entire day, and are joined in the early evening by warm meat loaf and noodles, and probably some fried ham announcing the start of the second meal of the day. Later still, after the gifts have been opened and the guests begin thinking of going home, a third round of food is brought out for those who may still feel hungry. Surprisingly, many do. These are hard-working farm people with huge appetites. Besides, who could resist this fare? The Amish are accustomed to good food all the time, but a wedding feast becomes something of a culinary competition where only the best will do.

To the Amish, a wedding symbolizes the creation of a new family, which not only helps assure the continuation of their way of life, but follows a biblical exhortation that is central to their religion: "Be fruitful and multiply." But although it is against their religion to recruit converts, it is also against their belief to influence their children to follow in their religious footsteps. Although Amish youngsters aren't forbidden to go to movies, hang out in shopping malls or patronize roadside diners, few of them actually do, but not because it is against the rules of the faith of their fathers. Until they become teenagers and eligible for baptism, they are quite free to live outside the church's rules. Even when they have announced a desire to become baptized and join the church, everything possible is done to make sure they understand what such a thing means, and they are given every chance to choose a less demanding life outside the church. There is no decision facing any young person in any religion on the face of the earth that carries more responsibility, because the Amish fervently believe that baptismal vows are a sacred covenant with God that can never be broken under any circumstances. From the moment a young person decides to join the church, the ministers deliver continuous warnings about what a significant step it is and they caution right through the moments leading up to the ceremony itself that it is far better never to make a vow than to make one and break it. There is no stigma attached to anyone who decides to heed the warning and stay unbaptized,

*Above: a horse-drawn family
buggy in Pennsylvania.*

spiritual ones. Ministers are chosen by lot, in the belief that divine intervention will guide the choice, and once chosen, a man will serve for the rest of his life. One of the promises a young man makes at baptism is a pledge to respond to a call to the ministry if it should come, and it usually comes quite unexpectedly. When the bishops hold lotteries, several names are chosen and the men are summoned to a special service. Before it begins, a slip of paper is inserted into a hymn book which is then mixed with the others to be used in the service. The candidate who picks up the marked book will become the chosen one and at the next gathering of the church, he can be expected to deliver the first sermon of the day, an inspirational and instructional message that will last an hour or more with no notes or any other reference beyond his own life experience. It is one of two sermons that are part of every Amish church service, a ritual that lasts from early morning through mid-afternoon and includes prayer and singing to punctuate the ministers' messages.

The weekly church services are usually followed by communal meals which, although not as extensive as the Amish wedding feasts, are an opportunity for housewives to display their culinary skills and to compete with others in the congregation for the acclaim of their neighbors. Not that any of them would admit it, of course, that would constitute committing the sin of pride, obviously contrary to the Amish religion. But if Amish cooks aren't boastful, and accept compliments with Christian humility, they do themselves proud every time they step into a kitchen. Their creations are as plain as their religion demands, but fancy enough to rate raves from those of us they call "English" or "city people." And although their accent is German, most of the dishes they are famous for can rightly be characterized as uniquely American. You'll find sauerkraut along the Rhine, and sauerbraten is regularly served in Bavaria along with pickled red cabbage, but none of it isn't quite the same as in Amish country. Can you find deviled crab in Cologne, scalloped sweet potatoes in Berlin, corn chowder in Bonn? And where in the world can you find mustard pickle at all like the Amish kind, or potato salad, potato pancakes, or even barbecued chicken? And who else but the Amish could produce a perfect shoofly pie?

Now the answer is that you can – thanks to this collection of authentic Amish recipes. The only secret ingredient that has to be added to any of them is love. To an Amish cook, every meal is a celebration, each an expression of love and affection.

although in spite of the admonitions, few back away from the responsibility.

According to the church's own figures, more than ninety percent of all youngsters raised by Amish parents go on to become church members themselves, and nearly all of the others wind up joining the similar, but far less restrictive, Mennonite religion. Boys generally take longer to commit themselves than girls – many Amish admit that their sons' decisions are often the result of romance because young people are forbidden to marry outside the faith and it is necessary to join the church before joining in wedlock. The average age of baptismal candidates is between sixteen and twenty, although many postpone the decision well into their twenties and sometimes beyond.

The ministers who guide them are recruited from the congregation itself, a practice that allowed them to easily transplant their religion into the New World without having to wait for trained clergy to follow them from the Old Country. The only requirement is that a minister must be a married man leading an exemplary life, and there are no rewards beyond the obvious

CHAPTER ONE

Soups

Above: plowing the soil in preparation for planting.
Many Plain People consider the use of tractors worldly
and horse-drawn farm machinery is still widely used.

With their wonderful traditions of simple and hearty foods, Amish families regularly serve nourishing and heart-warming soups. Plenty of home-grown vegetables are on hand to provide flavor, color, and variety, and soups are often a simple way to provide a supper for a large and hungry family, served, of course, with chunks of home-baked bread. They also have the advantage of being economical and a great way to use up leftovers, while still offering a solid and substantial dish.

German-Style Vegetable Soup

You can see both tradition and adaptation in this hearty soup which includes both German-style cabbage and New World corn and tomatoes.

1 pound beef bones
2 Tbsps oil
1 whole onion stuck with 1 clove
2 celery stalks, coarsely chopped
1 bay leaf
1 carrot, diced
2 cup corn kernels
2 cups shredded cabbage
1 large turnip, diced
2 cups lima beans
1 tsp all-purpose flour
½ cup milk
Salt and pepper
3 Tbsps chopped fresh parsley
2 cups chopped tomatoes

Brown the beef bones in the oil in a large stock pot. Add the onion, celery, and bay leaf and pour over enough water to cover by about 3 inches. Bring to a boil, skimming off any fat that floats to the surface. Simmer for about 2 hours. Strain and discard the bones, vegetables, and bay leaf.
Combine the stock with the carrot, corn, cabbage, turnip, and beans. Blend the flour and milk together until smooth and mix into the soup. Bring back to a boil, then simmer for 45 minutes. Add salt and pepper to taste and stir in the parsley and tomatoes. Cook another 15 minutes, or until the tomatoes are tender. Serve hot.
Serves 6.

Corn Chowder

The Native Americans believed that a crow carried a kernel of corn in one ear and a bean in the other from the great fields of the southwest, whence came all the corn and beans in the world. Never slow to absorb local crops into their cooking, corn is a very important ingredient in many Amish dishes.

3 Tbsps diced salt pork
1 Tbsp butter
1 medium onion, sliced
3 potatoes, finely diced
3 cups chicken stock
2 cups corn kernels
4 cups whole milk
Salt and pepper
3 Tbsps butter

Fry the salt pork in the butter until crispy. Remove the pieces and reserve. Add the onion to the fat and sauté until golden. Add the potatoes and stock and cook slowly until soft. Add the corn and milk, lower the heat and simmer until the corn is tender. Young corn takes 5 minutes. (Dried corn which has been freshened will take longer.) Add salt and pepper. Bring to a boil and remove from the heat. Add the butter. Stir up well and pour into soup plates or a tureen. Float the pork on top. Serves 6.

Split Pea Soup

Traditional methods of preserving are very important to the Amish, so dried pulses often feature in their cooking. This soup is delicious on its own, but is often served in inns and former coach houses with slices of locally-produced ham.

Favorite Supper Soup

Home-preserved hams often feature in Amish meals as the pork from pigs reared on the farms is readily available

1 pound soup beans
1 pound ham slice (bone in)
1 onion, chopped
1 pound can plum tomatoes, drained
2 potatoes, diced
1 tsp dried thyme
1 tsp chopped fresh parsley
Salt and pepper

Soak the beans overnight in cold water. Drain, place in a large pan and cover with fresh water. Add the ham slice and bring to a boil. Simmer for about 1 hour until the beans are tender, but not falling apart. Remove the ham and dice it. Discard the bone. Skim any fat from the surface of the beans. Return the ham to the beans and add the remaining ingredients. Simmer gently until the potatoes are soft. Serve at once with bread or rolls. Serves 4-6.

2 cups split peas
1 ham bone
1 small onion, finely chopped
1 bay leaf
3 Tbsps margarine
3 Tbsps all-purpose flour
Salt and pepper
2 cups milk
Chopped fresh mint (optional)
Croûtons, to serve

Soak the split peas overnight in enough water to cover. Drain, then place in a pan with 3 pints of cold water, the ham bone, onion, and bay leaf. Bring to a boil, then simmer until the peas are very tender. Remove the ham bone and scrape off any meat. Remove the bay leaf and purée the soup, if desired, then return the meat to the soup.
Melt the margarine and stir in the flour until smooth and well blended. Add salt and pepper and gradually stir in the milk. Cook, stirring constantly, until thickened. Add the split pea mixture and cook until very thick. Add the chopped mint, if using. If desired, other chopped herbs may also be used. Serve with croûtons and extra mint. Serves 4-6.

Above: in Amish families children are expected to work on the farm from an early age. Learning the skills necessary to run the farm is regarded as a vital part of their overall education.

Turkey Chowder

One of the most American of dishes, clam chowder is said to have French origins. The French fishermen used large kettles – chaudières – to cook the thick, creamy soup on the dock. While clam chowder may be one of the best known, chowders can be made with seafood or meat, but always contain lots of seasonal vegetables.

Brown Flour Potato Soup

Potatoes are available year-round and served in all sorts of ways, including this nourishing soup which is often given to any members of the family who are unwell. Dumplings are sometimes included to make a heartier dish.

2¼ cups diced potatoes
2½ cups water
2 Tbsps butter
5 Tbsps all-purpose flour
Salt and pepper

Put the potatoes and water in a large saucepan, add some salt and bring to a boil. Reduce the heat, then cover and simmer until just tender, about 10-15 minutes. Melt the butter in a skillet and stir in the flour. Stir constantly over a low heat until the mixture is a rich brown

Turkey bones
1 bay leaf
3 black peppercorns
1 blade of mace
1 onion, unpeeled
1 cup barley, rinsed
3 celery stalks, sliced
3 carrots, diced
1 cup cut green beans
1 cup corn kernels
2 Tbsps chopped fresh parsley

Use the carcass from a roast turkey and dice any leftover meat. Place the carcass in a large pot with the bay leaf, peppercorns, mace, and onion. Pour in enough cold water to cover the bones, and cover the pot. Bring to a boil, then simmer, partially covered, for about 2 hours. Strain and reserve the stock. Remove and reserve any meat from the bones.

Combine the strained stock, barley, celery, carrots, and green beans. Partially cover and bring to a boil. Cook for about 1 hour, or until the barley is tender. Add the corn after about 30 minutes cooking time. Stir in the chopped parsley and any diced turkey and heat through before serving. Serves 4-6.

color. Do not let the mixture burn. Measure the liquid from the potatoes and make up to 2½ cups if it has reduced. Gradually stir the liquid into the browned flour mixture, stirring constantly to prevent lumps from forming. When all the liquid is incorporated, add the potatoes and season to taste. Bring the soup to a boil, stirring constantly, and cook for 2-3 minutes. Serves 4.

Above: Plain People live a humble life. In some communities the ordnung, or traditional code of behavior, forbids the use of cars or electricity, and patterns of life continue as they have for centuries.

18

CHAPTER TWO

Appetizers

Above: two Amish farmers threshing wheat during the harvest. The rules regarding permitted and non-permitted pieces of technology are complex and vary from community to community.

With large families all contributing in their own ways to the life of the farm, Amish family meals need to be substantial and even the appetizers are homely and filling. Rather than rush backwards and forwards to the kitchen when serving meals, Amish cooks often present all the dishes together, steaming in the center of the table, so that the hungry diners can simply help themselves and not be bothered with waiting for courses.

Spiced Meat Pots

Nothing is wasted in the Amish kitchen – these meat pots can be made with any leftover cooked meats and stored for several days without spoiling.

2 cups cooked beef, pork or veal
2½ cups bouillon
¼ tsp ground cinnamon
¼ tsp ground nutmeg
¼ tsp ground ginger
1½ Tbsps chopped fresh thyme
1 Tbsp Worcestershire sauce
Salt and pepper
Pinch of cayenne pepper
1 Tbsp chopped fresh parsley
2 hard-boiled eggs, chopped
1½ cups butter
Small bay leaves
Toast or rolls to serve

Cook the meat and the bouillon until the meat is very tender. Mash with a fork and beat in the spices, thyme, Worcestershire sauce, salt, pepper, and cayenne pepper.

Fold in the parsley and the hard-boiled eggs, being careful not to break up the eggs. Spoon the mixture into small custard cups and chill.

Melt the butter, then turn up the heat until the butter foams, but does not brown. Watch it carefully. Remove from the heat and set aside until the butter fats sink to the bottom and the oil rises to the top. Some salt will float on the surface, but skim that off, then slowly pour off the clearer oil, leaving the milky fat sediments behind. Add these to cooked vegetables, if desired.

Spoon a layer of clarified butter over the surface of the potted meats. Chill until set. Garnish with bay leaves, then add more butter to cover the meat completely. Chill until ready to serve. Serve with toast or rolls. If the butter layer is unbroken, the potted meats will keep fresh for several days. Serves 4.

Above: a barn raising, a spectacular example of how Plain People draw together to help one another. Work begins at dawn and by the end of the day the barn will be completed. Beams are hewn and raised by hand and are joined by mortise and tenon.

Baked Stuffed Tomatoes

Eggs Goldenrod

This simple appetizer or snack has a tasty sauce that turns a straightforward meal into something more substantial.

1 Tbsp butter
1 Tbsp all-purpose flour
1 cup milk
Salt and white pepper
4 hard-boiled eggs
Toast
Paprika

Melt the butter in a small saucepan. Remove from the heat and add the flour. Stir in the milk and bring to a boil, stirring constantly until the sauce thickens. Add salt and pepper to taste.
Chop the egg whites and add them to the sauce. Spoon over hot toast on serving plates. Push the egg yolks through a sieve over the top of the sauce. Sprinkle lightly with paprika and serve immediately. Serves 4.

The Amish know exactly when to pick their fruit and vegetables by developing a feel for the ripeness of the produce. Consequently, tomato dishes such as this one always have great flavor because the tomatoes are picked when perfectly ripe.

6 large tomatoes
2 Tbsps butter, melted
2 Tbsps finely chopped fresh chives
1 Tbsp finely chopped fresh parsley
¼ tsp dried thyme
¼ tsp dried sage
2 cups breadcrumbs
½ cup finely grated cheese

Preheat the oven to 350° F. Remove the tomato stems and cut out the cores. Cut out the centers and scoop out the insides. Discard the seeds, chop the pulp and mix with the remaining ingredients, except the cheese. Fill the tomato shells with the stuffing ingredients. Place the tomatoes in a baking dish and sprinkle with the cheese. Bake in the oven for about 20-30 minutes, depending on the ripeness of the tomatoes. Serve hot. Serves 6.

Above: an Amish farmer tills his soil in time-honored fashion in preparation for planting. Most farm machinery is horse drawn and it is usual for an Amish farmer to own six horses or mules specifically for this purpose.

Savory Foldovers

Most Amish farms include a dairy herd, so fresh milk, butter, and cheeses feature regularly. Delicious hot or cold, these foldovers are perfect for suppers, lunch boxes or picnics, too.

2 cups all-purpose flour
½ pound butter or margarine
½ pound cream cheese
2 oz liver sausage or finely chopped ham
½ tsp dried dill
2 tsps Worcestershire sauce
Poppy seeds
Paprika

Sift the flour into a bowl and rub in the butter or margarine until the mixture resembles bread crumbs. Work in the cream cheese and chill overnight. Mix the liver sausage or ham with the dill and Worcestershire sauce. If desired, use a half quantity of ham and half liver sausage, adding half the dill and Worcestershire sauce to each for two different fillings.

Preheat the oven to 400°F. Lightly grease several baking sheets. Divide the dough into an even number of pieces. The foldovers can be small or large. Roll out each piece on a well-floured surface and cut circles with a cookie cutter.
Spread each circle with filling and fold over to make half circles, sealing the edges with a little water. Sprinkle with poppy seeds and paprika, one for each different filling, if desired. Place on baking sheets and bake until browned, about 15 minutes. The foldovers may be shaped in advance and kept chilled until ready to bake. Serve hot or cold. Makes about 28.

Above: a group of Amish men gather at an outdoor sale of machinery. The winter months on the farm are relatively slack and this is an important time for auctions and sales, both of machinery and animals as well as land and buildings. Right: a farmer preparing his land.

26

Main Courses

*Above: children playing outside a one-room Amish
schoolhouse during recess. Schoolhouses such as these
are usually built on land donated by a local farmer
and are paid for and run by parents.*

Combining the culinary traditions brought from
Germany with the locally available ingredients,
Amish cooks employ simple techniques with a robust flair.
What all these dishes have in common is that they use
fresh farm ingredients to create substantial dishes for a
hungry family. After a hard day on the farm, when all
members of the family, except the very youngest, will have
worked hard it is such dishes as meat pies, casseroles and
roasts that are needed to fill empty stomachs.

Fried Chicken
with Gravy

A favorite at threshing time when the cook may have to serve up to twenty-two work-weary farmers, this dish complements the flavor of the chicken with a creamy herb gravy.

3-4 pound chicken
1 cup all-purpose flour
Pinch of rubbed sage
Pinch of dried thyme
Pinch of paprika
Salt and pepper
Milk
Oil for frying
1 cup milk or half and half
Watercress or fresh parsley sprigs to garnish
Mashed potatoes and vegetables to serve

Cut the chicken into 6 pieces, breasts with wings attached, thighs, and drumsticks. If desired, cut the back into 2 pieces.
Mix together about 1 cup of flour with a good pinch of the herbs, paprika, salt, and pepper. Dip the chicken in milk then coat in flour, shaking off the excess. Reserve 1 tablespoon of the flour.
Heat enough oil in a large skillet to come at least halfway up the sides of the chicken pieces. When hot, add the chicken, bone-side down first. Fry the chicken over moderate heat until golden brown. Turn over and fry the other side. Lower the heat and cook slowly, with the oil barely bubbling, until chicken is tender and cooked through. Turn once or twice to ensure even cooking. Drain the cooked chicken on paper towels.
Remove all but 2 tablespoons of the oil from the pan, add the reserved flour and cook until a pale gold color. Gradually whisk in the milk or half and half. Bring to a boil and cook until thickened. Serve the chicken garnished with watercress or parsley. Accompany with mashed potatoes, vegetables, and the gravy. Serves 4-6.

Above: a reconstruction of an eighteenth-century Amish kitchen. Food has always played an important part in Amish family life and the tradition of hearty, sustaining food, brought by the German immigrants in the early eighteenth century, remains to this day.

Chicken Pot Pie

Chickens are always available on Amish farms and are the perfect solution to feeding unexpected guests. This filling dish is often served in quantity when friends and neighbors are helping with silo filling or haymaking.

Home-Barbecued Chicken

Great for barbecuing or broiling, this chicken has a spicy sweet and sour glaze.

1/2 cup tomato ketchup
3 Tbsps vinegar
3 Tbsps brown sugar
2 tsps Worcestershire sauce
1/2 tsp onion salt
1/4 tsp garlic powder
1/3 cup oil
4 broiler chicken halves

Combine the ketchup, vinegar, brown sugar, Worcestershire sauce, onion salt, garlic powder, and oil. Heat gently until just boiling. Cool completely.
Grease the broiler pan and rack and preheat the broiler. Brush the chicken skin with the oil and broil about 5 inches away from the heat until the skin begins to crisp. Turn the chicken over and broil again until beginning to brown. Turn the chicken over again, lower the heat and baste with the sauce several times until the chicken is cooked, about 20 minutes.
Serve the chicken with any remaining sauce. Serves 8.

4 Tbsps margarine
1/2 onion, chopped
4 Tbsps all-purpose flour
2 cups chicken bouillon
3 pounds chicken, cooked, boned and cut into chunks
1 cup cooked, diced potatoes
1/2 cup corn kernels
1/2 cup cooked, diced carrot
1/2 cup peas, blanched
1/2 cup cut green beans, blanched
1 Tbsp chopped fresh parsley
1/3 tsp rubbed sage

TOPPING
1 1/2 cups all-purpose flour
1 tsp baking powder
1/4 tsp salt
1/2 cup sour cream

Heat the margarine in a saucepan and add the onion. Cook slowly until softened. Add the flour and cook to a pale golden color. Stir in the bouillon and bring to a boil. Cook until thickened, stirring constantly. Combine with the chicken and vegetables. Add the parsley and sage, and spoon into a deep pie plate or a casserole dish. Preheat the oven to 400°F. Combine the flour, baking powder, and salt. Gradually work in the sour cream. Press out on a floured surface with your hands; do not roll. Cut into rounds with a cookie cutter. Place on top of the chicken mixture. Bake for 20 minutes, or until the chicken is hot and the topping has risen and browned. Serve immediately. Serves 4-6.

Salmon Loaf

Salmon caught in the eastern rivers used to be a Fourth of July favorite. Canning the local salmon in Amish kitchens preserves the delicate fish, and leads to interesting recipes such as this variation on the meat loaf.

1 pound can salmon
1 cup cracker crumbs
1/2 cup milk
1 Tbsp butter, melted
2 eggs, beaten
Salt and pepper
Fresh parsley sprigs to garnish

Preheat the oven to 350°F. Grease a bread pan well. Mix the salmon, cracker crumbs, milk, butter, beaten eggs, and a pinch of salt and pepper. Spoon the mixture into the pan and smooth the top. Cover with buttered foil and bake in the oven for about 30 minutes. Uncover the pan after about 15 minutes to allow the top to brown. Garnish with parsley and serve hot. Delicious with cucumbers in sour cream. Serves 4.

Right: two Amish boys pause for a moment's rest.

Country-Style Roast Turkey

This is definitely a celebration dish for a wedding, family gathering or, of course, Thanksgiving. The turkey is simply but succulently cooked and complemented by a homemade sausage meat stuffing.

3 Tbsps butter, melted
8 oz sausage meat
1 small onion, finely chopped
2 celery stalks, chopped
4 cups cubed bread, dried
1 tsp salt
Pinch of black pepper
1/4 tsp poultry seasoning
1 Tbsp chopped fresh parsley
1 egg, beaten
10-12 pound turkey
1/2 cup shortening
1/2 cup flour
Mashed potatoes or sweet potatoes and vegetables to serve

Heat the butter in a pan and add the sausage meat. Cook slowly for about 15 minutes, breaking up the meat with a fork. When the meat is nearly cooked, add the onion and celery and cook until the meat is done. Meanwhile, soak the bread in bouillon or water until starting to soften. Combine the bread with the sausage mixture and the salt, pepper, poultry seasoning, parsley, and egg. Preheat the oven to 450°F.

Remove the giblets from the turkey and rinse out the cavity. Fill with the stuffing and put any remaining mixture under the flap of skin at the neck end. Truss or place foil over the opening to keep the stuffing moist. Mix the shortening and flour and rub over the legs, breast, and wings. Place the turkey in a roasting pan and cover with a tight fitting lid. Roast for 15 minutes. Reduce the heat to 400°F and roast for 3½ hours, or until tender and the juices run clear. Uncover during the last half of the roasting time.
Make a gravy as in the recipe for Fried Chicken with Gravy, using some of the turkey fat and the pan juices. Carve the turkey and serve it with the gravy, mashed potatoes or sweet potatoes, and vegetables. Serves 8-10.

Above: a peaceful day on a typical Amish farm. Farming is not seen as a job by the Amish, but a way of life, and an important link with their faith.

34

Beef Stew

At the busiest times of the farming season, a wholesome stew with fresh seasonal vegetables can be left to cook unattended while the cook sees to other tasks around the farm. Stews and casseroles are popular, too, at quilting bees, when the women get together to sew and share the latest news.

2½ pounds chuck or round steak
3 Tbsps oil
2 onions
2 small turnips, diced
3 carrots, diced
3 potatoes, diced
2 celery stalks, sliced
½ cup all-purpose flour
½ tsp salt
¼ tsp black pepper
4 cups water
1 bay leaf
1 cup peas
Potato dumplings, noodles or mashed potatoes to serve

Cut the meat into 2-inch pieces, trimming off the fat. Heat the oil in a large pot and fry the meat in small batches until well browned. Remove and set aside. Add the onions, turnips, carrots, potatoes, and celery to the pot and cook slowly to brown lightly. Remove and set aside with the meat.

If necessary, add more oil to the pot. Add the flour and cook slowly until a good, rich brown color. Return the meat and vegetables to the pan and add the salt, pepper, water, and bay leaf. Bring to a boil, then reduce the heat and simmer the stew for about 2 hours, or until the meat and vegetables are tender.

Remove the bay leaf and add the peas to the stew. Cook for about 15 minutes, or until the peas are tender. Serve with potato dumplings, noodles or mashed potatoes.
Serves 4-6.

Above: an Amish buggy and farm scene. Right: harrowing the land in preparation for the spring planting.

Sauerbraten

With its German ancestry quite clear from the name, this is thought to be the forerunner of that famous American staple, the pot roast.

4 pound piece round or chuck steak
2 cups cider vinegar
2 bay leaves
1 tsp dried thyme
½ tsp black pepper
6 whole cloves
½ tsp salt
½ cup all-purpose flour
1 tsp ground allspice
4 Tbsps oil
4 carrots, quartered
4 small onions, quartered
4 parsnips or turnips, quartered
12 gingersnaps, finely crushed
1 Tbsp brown sugar
Fresh parsley sprigs to garnish
Boiled or mashed potatoes to serve

Place the meat in a large bowl. Mix the vinegar, bay leaves, thyme, pepper, and cloves, and pour over the meat. Add enough water to cover the meat completely. Keep in the refrigerator for two days. Drain the meat and reserve the vinegar mixture.
Pat the meat dry with paper towels. Mix together the salt, flour, and allspice and rub into the surface of the meat on all sides. Heat the oil in a large pot or deep skillet. When hot, brown the meat well on all sides.
Remove the meat and add the carrots, onions, and parsnips or turnips, brown lightly and return the meat to the pan. Pour over 2 cups of the vinegar mixture. Cover the pan and cook over a low heat for about 2 hours, stirring occasionally.
When the meat is tender, remove it to a serving dish along with the vegetables. Skim any fat from the surface of the cooking liquid and stir in the crushed gingersnaps and the sugar. Cook for about 10 minutes then spoon some of the sauce over the meat. Garnish with fresh parsley. Serve the rest of the sauce separately and accompany with boiled or mashed potatoes. Serves 6-8.

Roast Pork

Roasts are often served on Sundays and for special celebrations. This one is given a hint of the unusual with a sprinkling of ground ginger.

6 pound pork loin roast
Salt and pepper
1 tsp ground ginger
All-purpose flour
2 onions, sliced
Potato dumplings and vegetables to serve

Place the pork in a roasting pan and season well with salt and pepper. Rub over the ground ginger and dust with flour.
Preheat the oven to 400°F. Cook the meat at this temperature until brown on the surface. Lower the temperature to 350°F and add the onions and 1 cup of water to the pan. Cook for about 25 minutes to the pound at the lower temperature, basting every 15 minutes.
When the pork is cooked through, remove it to a carving dish and leave it to stand for 15 minutes. Skim all but 1 tablespoon of the fat from the pan and leave the meat juices and browned onions. Add 2 tablespoons of flour to the pan and pour in 1½ cups of water. Cook slowly until the gravy boils and thickens, stirring constantly. Carve the meat and serve with the gravy, potato dumplings, and vegetables. Serves 6-8.

Above: Mascot Grist Mill, Lancaster County, Pennsylvania.

Meat Loaf

Originally with a seasonal aspect, meat loaf was one of the dishes cooked when there were no more chickens available. Depending on the time of year, it would be served with scalloped potatoes, macaroni and cheese or new potatoes with brown butter.

3 eggs
2 large potatoes
3 pounds lean ground beef
1 onion, finely chopped
Salt and pepper
1 tsp chopped fresh parsley
2 slices of bread, made into crumbs
1 tsp Worcestershire sauce
¼ cup all-purpose flour
¼ pound sliced bacon
Fresh parsley sprigs to garnish

Hard-boil the eggs, shell them, and keep them in cold water. Peel the potatoes and cut them into chunks. Boil until tender, then mash them and leave to cool.
Combine the mashed potatoes with the ground beef, onion, salt and pepper to taste, parsley, breadcrumbs, and Worcestershire sauce.
Divide the meat mixture in half and shape each half into a thick rectangle. Drain the hard-boiled eggs, pat dry and dust lightly with flour. Place the eggs down the center of one of the meat rectangles. Place the other on top and mold the meat around the eggs to cover them completely.
Preheat the oven to 400°F. Wrap the slices of bacon around the meat loaf to cover and tie them on with string. Place in a roasting pan and bake for about 1½ hours, or until the meat is completely cooked. Serve hot or cold, garnished with fresh parsley. Serves 6-8.

Glazed Ham

The sugar and mustard coating gives a crisp and sweet-savory crust to this delicious ham.

10 pound ham
Whole cloves
1 cup brown sugar
1 Tbsp dry mustard
1½ Tbsps all-purpose flour
Canned pineapple slices

Place the ham in a large pot and cover with water. Bring slowly to a boil, then simmer for 1 hour. Allow to cool in the water, then remove the ham and pour off the water. Using a sharp knife, remove the rind from the ham.
Preheat the oven to 325°F. Score the fat at 1-inch intervals and stick with cloves. Combine the brown sugar, dry mustard, and flour and press on all sides to a thickness of about 1½ inches. Pour the juice from the pineapple over the top of the ham. Place on the pineapple slices.

Bake for about 25 minutes to the pound, basting often. Lower the oven temperature to 300°F about 15 minutes before the end of cooking time. Coat with more brown sugar mixture and bake for the last 15 minutes without basting for a crisp glaze.
Allow the ham to stand for 15 minutes before carving.
Serves 8-10.

Right: a pensive moment for a group of Amish men at a sale.

Kraut and Chops

With recipes brought with them from Europe, Amish cooks prepare sauerkraut during the summer glut when they can and preserve many items for use during the winter. Sweetened with apples and brown sugar, and with the tang of caraway, the kraut makes a perfect foil for pork chops.

Smoked Sausage with Gravy

A very Germanic dish with the rich smoked sausage fried to a crisp and served with onion gravy.

1 Tbsp margarine
1½ pound smoked sausage
1 onion, sliced
½ pound mushrooms, sliced
1 Tbsp all-purpose flour
1½ cups beef bouillon
Chopped fresh dill
Sauerkraut or potatoes to serve

Heat the margarine in a skillet and when hot add the sausage. Cook slowly, turning frequently until browned.
Remove the sausage from the skillet and keep it warm. Add the onion to the pan and cook until golden brown. Add the mushrooms and cook until softened. Place with the sausage.
If necessary, add more margarine to the skillet. Stir in the flour and cook until lightly browned. Stir in the bouillon and bring to a boil.

2 pound can sauerkraut
3 Tbsps oil
8 pork chops
2 apples, cored and sliced
2 Tbsps brown sugar
3 Tbsps caraway seeds

Drain the sauerkraut well and rinse in cold water. Leave to dry.
Heat the oil in a large skillet and brown the chops slowly on both sides. Remove and keep them warm.
Combine the sauerkraut with the apples, brown sugar, and caraway seeds. Add to the pan and cook slowly until the pan juices have been absorbed. Add about 1½ cups water and return the chops to the pan. Cover the pan and cook slowly until the chops are done and the water has evaporated. Watch the sauerkraut carefully and add more water if necessary during cooking to prevent burning. Serves 4-8.

Cook, stirring constantly, until thickened.
Slice the sausage into serving portions and return it to the pan along with onions and mushrooms to heat through. Sprinkle with chopped dill and serve with sauerkraut or potatoes. Serves 4.

Above: many Amish families sell surplus produce from their farms and gardens at the local farmer's market. Their produce is valued for its high quality and excellent flavor.

Paprika Schnitzel

Pounded until very thin, these veal or pork steaks are cooked in traditional European style then given a unique twist with a sauce of peppers, tomato, and sour cream.

4 veal cutlets or pork steaks
½ cup all-purpose flour
Salt and pepper
2 Tbsps oil
1 small onion, finely chopped
1 red bell pepper, sliced
1 tsp paprika
1 cup tomato sauce
1 cup sour cream
Dumplings, potatoes, or noodles to serve

Pound the veal or pork between sheets of wax paper until meat is very thin. Mix the flour with a good pinch of salt and pepper and coat the meat, shaking off the excess. Heat the oil in a large skillet and when hot add the meat. Fry on both sides until golden brown, about 5 minutes each side. Remove to a plate and keep them warm.
Add the onion and pepper to the pan and cook slowly until softened but not browned, about 5 minutes. Stir in the paprika and cook for 1 minute. Add the tomato sauce and return the cutlets to the pan. Cover and simmer for about 20 minutes, or until the meat is tender.
Remove the meat and vegetables to a serving dish. Stir the sour cream into the pan and cook gently to heat through. Do not let the sour cream boil. Spoon over the meat and serve with dumplings, potatoes, or noodles.

Amish Omelet

A simple but hearty meal, you can choose your own omelet ingredients but bacon, ham, mushrooms, and onions are traditional.

¼ pound bacon, diced
¼ pound ham, diced
¼ pound mushrooms, sliced
6 green onions, sliced
4 eggs
4 Tbsps milk
Salt and pepper

Fry the bacon in a heavy skillet until crisp. Remove and drain on paper towels. Add the ham and mushrooms to the pan and cook until the mushrooms are tender, then return the bacon to the pan and add the onions.
Beat the eggs and the milk with a pinch of salt and pepper. Pour over the mixture in the pan and cook for about 3 minutes, stirring frequently until beginning to set. Allow to cook slowly without stirring until the eggs are set. Serve immediately with toast and sliced tomatoes. Serves 2.

Above: Sgraffito plate. Right: an Amish couple, caught in the rain, wend their way homeward.

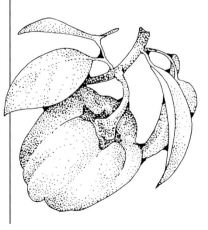

44

Cabbage Rolls

Recipes that are tasty, nutritious and make good use of a variety of ingredients are often handed down through Amish generations. Cabbage is a winter favorite often served with beef liver.

2 Tbsps oil
1 onion, finely chopped
1 can condensed tomato soup
1 Tbsp vinegar
1 tsp sugar
1 Tbsp chopped fresh parsley
2 tsps chopped fresh dill
6 large cabbage leaves
½ pound ground pork
½ pound ground beef
⅓ cup uncooked rice
2 celery stalks, chopped
Salt and pepper
1 egg, beaten
Fresh dill, to garnish

Heat the oil in a saucepan and add the onion. Cook slowly until softened. Stir in the tomato soup and half a can of water. Add the vinegar, sugar, parsley, and dill. Bring to a boil, then simmer for about 10 minutes. If very thick, add more water. Set aside.

If the cabbage leaves have thick spines, pare them down slightly to make them easier to roll. Blanch the leaves a few minutes in boiling water to soften them slightly. Drain and pat dry.
Combine the ground meats with the rice, celery, salt and pepper, and egg, mixing well.
Put 2 tablespoons of the meat mixture into each cabbage leaf and roll up, tucking in the sides. Secure each roll with a toothpick. Place the rolls in a saucepan. Season the sauce to taste and pour it over the rolls. Cover the pan and place over a low heat. Cook slowly until the meat is done and the rice is tender, at least 2 hours. Serve immediately, garnished with fresh dill. Serves 4-6.

Above: a contemporary kitchen scene. The lovingly crafted wooden cabinet and the beautifully carved molds that adorn the walls are evidence of the woodworking skills of their Amish creator.

46

CHAPTER FOUR

Vegetables, Salads, and Pickles

*Above: two family buggies standing at the roadside as
their owners stop to exchange news. Though some
Amish are permitted to use the phone, its use is
restricted to business calls.*

*A*ll manner of fresh vegetables are on hand for the
Amish cook and she uses them according to season,
picking them at their most perfect for ripeness and flavor,
an art which comes with experience. Canning and
preserving vegetables to last through the winter is vital,
and many pickling recipes are handed down through the
generations of families. Canning jars in the storeroom
hold everything from string beans, beets, carrots, and
tomatoes to jams, apple preserves, and pickles.

Lettuce Salad

Lettuce is more versatile than we often give it credit for. Not just for cold salads, it is served at Amish meals with bacon and a creamy egg sauce.

1 head Romaine lettuce, washed
8 strips of bacon
2 Tbsps butter
½ cup heavy cream
2 eggs
½ tsp salt
1 Tbsp sugar
4 Tbsps cider vinegar
Pepper
Paprika

Tear the lettuce into large pieces and place in a bowl. Dice the strips of bacon and fry slowly in a skillet until some of the fat renders. Raise the heat and cook the bacon until crisp. Scatter over the lettuce.
Melt the butter in the pan with any remaining bacon fat. Stir in the cream and bring to a boil, then simmer gently. Beat the eggs with the salt, sugar, vinegar, and pepper. Pour into the hot cream mixture and cook gently, stirring constantly, until the consistency is that of thick custard. Pour over the lettuce and bacon, and toss to coat. Sprinkle with paprika and serve immediately as a side dish with meat or poultry. Serves 4.

Cucumber Cream Salad

Using the American love of sweet and sour flavor combinations, this makes the best of fresh farm cucumbers and has a bite which is the perfect accompaniment to roast meats.

1 large cucumber, thinly sliced
Salt
½ cup sour cream
1 Tbsp vinegar
Pepper
1 tsp chopped fresh dill
Paprika
Fresh dill sprigs to garnish

Place the cucumber slices in a colander and sprinkle with salt. Leave to drain for several hours. Rinse well in cold water and pat dry on paper towels. Place in a bowl.
Mix the sour cream, vinegar, pepper, and dill together and combine with the cucumbers. Sprinkle with paprika and garnish with sprigs of dill. Serves 4-6.

Above: two young boys helping their father with the crops. From an early age Amish children are expected to help out on the farm.

50

Sauerkraut

One of the most famous German dishes brought from Europe is still prepared today, and is served here with a sweetening of apple and sugar. The popularity of sauerkraut is widespread in many states settled by Germans; in Waynesville, Ohio they even hold an annual Sauerkraut Festival.

2 Tbsps oil
1 onion, sliced
1 quart canned sauerkraut, rinsed
1 potato, coarsely grated
1 apple, peeled, cored, and sliced
Brown sugar
1 Tbsp caraway seeds

Heat the oil in a large pot and add the onion. Cook until golden. Stir in the sauerkraut and cook for about 5 minutes. Add the potato and apple, and cover with boiling water. Cook slowly for about 30 minutes. Taste and add brown sugar as desired. Stir in the caraway seeds. Cover the pan and cook very slowly for another 30 minutes. Serve with duck, pork, or sausages. Serves 4-6.

Beets and Eggs

When a glut of produce is available on the farm, preserving comes into its own, and this is a traditional way with beets and eggs.

6-16 whole beets (depending on size), peeled
½ cup cider vinegar
½ cup cold water
¼ cup sugar
1 bay leaf
3 allspice berries
Small piece of cinnamon stick
6 hard-boiled eggs
Lettuce leaves
Sour cream
Chopped fresh dill
Rye bread and butter to serve

Place the whole beets in a deep saucepan. Mix the vinegar, cold water, and sugar together. Add the bay leaf, allspice berries, and cinnamon and pour over the beets. Cover the pan and bring slowly to a boil. Cook rapidly for about 10 minutes then remove from the heat. Let the beets stand in the liquid for several days. Remove the beets and store them in an airtight container in a cool place.

Peel the hard-boiled eggs and add to the beet liquid. Let the eggs pickle for about 2 days in a cool place. To serve, slice or cube the beets. Cut the eggs in halves or quarters and arrange on lettuce leaves. Add a spoonful of sour cream and sprinkle with dill. Serve with rye bread and butter. Serves 6.

Above: the family wash hanging out to dry outside an Amish homestead in Lancaster County, Pennsylvania. Right: a young boy giving one of the farm horses its evening feed.

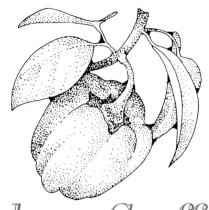

Cabbage-Stuffed Peppers

The sweet-and-sour mixture of vinegar, mustard and sugar lifts the flavor of Old World cabbage baked inside New World peppers.

6 sweet red bell peppers
3 Tbsps butter or margarine
1 small onion, finely sliced
1 head white or green cabbage, shredded
1 Tbsp chopped fresh dill
2 tsps mild mustard
2 Tbsps vinegar
2 Tbsps sugar
Salt and pepper
Fresh dill to garnish

Cut off the tops of the peppers and remove the seeds and cores. Blanch the peppers and tops in boiling water for about 5 minutes. Remove and drain upside down on paper towels.

Heat the butter or margarine in a large saucepan and add the onion and cabbage. Cook for about 10 minutes, stirring frequently. Stir in the chopped dill, mustard, vinegar, and sugar. Taste and add more vinegar or sugar as necessary, together with salt and pepper.

Preheat the oven to 300°F. Spoon the cabbage filling into the peppers and replace the tops. Place in a tight-fitting baking dish. Pour in a little water and cover the dish with foil. Bake for 35-45 minutes, or until the peppers are just tender. Garnish with fresh dill and serve hot as an accompaniment to meat. Serves 6.

Pepper Relish

The old traditions of pickling extend to the "new" crops discovered when the European peoples settled in America.

5 small onions
8 sweet green bell peppers
8 sweet red bell peppers
2 cups white distilled vinegar
¾ cup sugar
1½ Tbsps salt
2 Tbsps celery seed

Cut the onions into small dice about ¼-inch square. Cut the peppers in half, remove the cores and seeds and cut into dice the same size as the onions. Place in a large bowl and pour over boiling water. Let stand for 5 minutes then drain. Cover with more boiling water and leave to stand for 10 minutes. Drain overnight in a colander.

Combine the onions and peppers with the vinegar, sugar, salt, and celery seeds in a large pot. Bring to a boil, then cook rapidly for about 20 minutes. While still hot, pour into sterilized jars and seal tightly. Store for several weeks before serving. Serves 6-8.

Right: Lancaster County, Pennsylvania. The Amish are very successful at maintaining their own way of life, despite the influences of the outside world.

Potato Salad

Every farmer loves potatoes, according to Amish tradition, and this traditional salad makes a filling side dish.

Potato Dumplings

The German love of traditional, substantial food shows its influence in this filling and nutritious dish. Potatoes have always been a staple ingredient for the Amish, who still prepare the potato dumplings so popular in Southern Germany.

10 slices white bread, crusts trimmed
1 onion, grated
2 eggs, beaten
½ tsp finely chopped fresh parsley
½ tsp chopped fresh dill
6 potatoes, peeled
Salt and pepper
Pinch of grated nutmeg

10 red potatoes, boiled in their skins
2 celery stalks, thinly sliced
1 small onion, finely chopped
1 Tbsp chopped fresh parsley
3 hard-boiled eggs, sliced
1½ cups mayonnaise
1 Tbsp mustard
Pinch of salt and pepper
1 pimiento, chopped
2 baby dill pickles, sliced
Paprika
Fresh parsley sprigs to garnish

Peel the potatoes while still warm. Dice them and place in a large bowl with the celery, onion, and parsley. Add the hard-boiled eggs, reserving a few slices for the top of the salad.

Mix together the mayonnaise, mustard, salt and pepper. Add the pimiento and dill pickles to the salad and combine with the mayonnaise, coating the ingredients thoroughly. Place the egg slices on top and sprinkle with paprika. Garnish with fresh parsley. Serves 4-6.

Bring a large pot of water to a boil. Soak the bread in cold water and squeeze out as much water as possible. Mix the bread with the onion, eggs, parsley, and dill. Grate the potatoes finely and mix into the bread mixture. Add salt and pepper to taste and a pinch of nutmeg.

Shape the mixture into balls with floured hands. Drop the dumplings into the boiling water and cook for about 15 minutes. When the dumplings are cooked, they will rise to the surface. You may need to turn them several times. Remove from the water and drain on paper towels. Serve with stews. Serves 6.

Above: a young Amish boy and girl traveling in a courting buggy. In the Amish community sixteen is a landmark age. It signals the beginning of rumspringa, *or the running around time, when parents choose not to notice high-spirited behavior.*

Creamy Lima Beans

Lima beans are one of the crops inherited from the Indians when the Amish set up their homes in Pennsylvania and the surrounding areas. The beans are used fresh, and also dried so that they can be stored throughout the winter.

1 pound lima beans
4 potatoes, diced
2 oz smoked ham
1¼ cups half and half
1 Tbsp butter
1 Tbsp chopped fresh parsley
Grated nutmeg

Above: a complex of farm buildings in Lancaster County, Pennsylvania. Amish farms are passed from father to son and when parents move from the main farmhouse, leaving it to one of their sons and his family, they move to the "gossdawdy" house, which is set slightly apart from the main house or attached as an annex to it. Right: an Amish elder.

Remove the lima beans from their pods, if necessary. (Frozen lima beans may also be used.) Place the beans and potatoes in cold water, cover and bring slowly to a boil. Simmer, half covered, until tender, about 15-20 minutes.

Drain the vegetables and return to the pan. Add the ham and pour in the half and half. Add the butter and heat until almost boiling. Stir in the parsley and sprinkle with nutmeg to serve. Serves 4.

Mustard Pickles

Preserving a range of summer vegetables in a thick mustard sauce is a popular Amish recipe. Many Amish families sell their produce through local markets and the pickles and preserves are particularly popular items.

Pickled Red Cabbage

Pickles are the perfect way to keep the goodness of the summer through the winter cold, and cabbage is a particular favorite brought from Germany.

Red cabbage, shredded
Salt
White distilled vinegar
Sugar
Pepper, grated nutmeg, cinnamon, allspice and celery seed
Granny Smith apples, cored and sliced (optional)
Fresh parsley sprigs to garnish

Use as many heads of cabbage as you like. Place the shredded cabbage in a large bowl and sprinkle liberally with salt. Leave overnight. Drain all the moisture from the cabbage then leave for several hours at room temperature.
Pour enough vinegar over the cabbage to cover, then strain it off into a pan. Add 1 cup of sugar for every gallon of vinegar. Add a good pinch of each of the spices and the celery seed. Boil for 7-8 minutes, then pour over the cabbage. Spoon into stoneware jars or glass storage

2 cups diced cucumbers
2 cups pearl onions, peeled
2 cups diced green bell peppers
1 cup salt
2 heads cauliflower, cut into small florets
4 cups distilled white vinegar
1 cup all-purpose flour
1½ cups sugar
1 cup mild mustard
2 Tbsps celery seed
1 Tbsp turmeric

Place the cucumbers, onions, and peppers in a colander and sprinkle with the salt. Leave to stand overnight. Rinse and cover with water. Bring to a boil, then simmer until thoroughly cooked. Drain well and, when cold, mix with the cauliflower.
Mix ½ cup of the vinegar with the flour to make a thick paste. Bring the remaining vinegar to the boil. Mix the sugar, mustard, celery seed, and turmeric into the vinegar and flour paste and whisk into the boiling vinegar. Add the vegetables and cook until beginning to thicken. Remove from the heat and pour into sterilized jars. Seal and store for several weeks before using.

jars and cover. Store in a cool place for several weeks before using. If desired, add a sliced apple for every 2 cups of cabbage just before serving. Garnish with fresh parsley. Serves 4-6.

Above: a grain threshing team at work on an Amish farm in Lancaster County. Grain teams move from farm to farm during July when the wheat crop is ready for harvesting. The threshing machines that are used, once a common sight all over America, are now used only by Plain People.

CHAPTER FIVE

Baking

Above: an Amish farmer cultivating his fields with the aid of his two small sons. The discipline of hard work is a fundamental part of Amish philosophy and hard toil is held in high regard.

With wheat, rye, barley, and corn all grown on the farms, bread-making is a daily activity. The dough is made and left to rise while the laundry is washed, then baked once the clothes have been hung out to dry. Stone ovens were once built behind the farmhouses, specially designed to be wide enough to hold one large log. When the fire burned low, the embers were raked over until red hot and ready for baking. Helping their mothers every day, the girls learn the family recipes and secrets to pass on to their own children. And with hungry families to feed, baking pies and desserts is a regular activity, although families now tend not to offer a choice of so many desserts at one meal as they used to, when it was customary to offer "seven sweets and seven sours"!

Shoofly Pie

Uniquely Pennsylvania Dutch, this wonderful pie with its thick molasses and fragrant spices is supposed to have got its name from the fact that it is so sweet they have to shoo away the flies while it is cooling on the verandah. Few Amish cooks use a recipe, instead they add the molasses until the mixture is "just so."

PASTRY
1 cup all-purpose flour
¼ tsp salt
⅓ cup shortening
1 Tbsp butter
Milk

CRUMB MIXTURE
¾ cup all-purpose flour
½ tsp cinnamon
Pinch of nutmeg, ground cloves, and ginger
Pinch of salt
½ cup brown sugar
2 Tbsps shortening

FILLING
½ Tbsp baking soda
¾ cup boiling water
½ cup molasses
1 egg yolk, well beaten

TO SERVE
Whipped cream or vanilla ice cream

To prepare the pie crust, blend the flour, salt, shortening, and butter until the mixture resembles bread crumbs. Mix in enough milk to form a firm dough. Chill for about 10 minutes, then roll out and line an 8-inch pie plate. To make the crumb mixture, combine the flour with the spices, salt, and sugar. Blend in the shortening until the mixture forms coarse crumbs.

To make the filling, dissolve the baking soda in the boiling water and blend in the molasses and egg yolk thoroughly. Preheat the oven to 400°F. Fill the pie with alternating layers of the crumb and filling mixture, ending with crumbs. Bake until the crust edges start to brown. Lower the temperature to 350°F and bake for about 20 minutes, or until the filling is set. Serve warm or cold with whipped cream or vanilla ice cream. Serves 6.

Above: a contemporary Amish kitchen. Large families are still the norm among Plain People, and the kitchen, the heart of family life, has to be large enough to accommodate them.

Cottage Pudding

A simple dish with the tang of orange in the pudding and lemon in the sauce.

½ cup butter or margarine
1 cup sugar
1 egg, beaten
2½ cups all-purpose flour
4 tsps baking powder
¼ tsp salt
1 cup milk
Grated rind of 1 orange
2 Tbsps currants

PUDDING SAUCE
½ cup sugar
1 Tbsp all-purpose flour
Juice of 1 orange
Boiling water
2 Tbsps butter
1 Tbsp lemon juice

Preheat the oven to 350° F. Cream the butter or margarine together until light and fluffy. Beat in the egg. Sift the dry ingredients and add them, alternating with the milk, to the creamed butter. Stir in the grated orange rind and the currants. Squeeze the orange juice for the sauce. Pour the pudding mixture into a well greased cake pan and bake for about 35 minutes.
To make the sauce, mix the sugar and flour together in the top part of a double boiler. Add enough boiling water to the orange juice to make 2 cups of liquid. Gradually beat into the sugar and flour. Place the mixture over simmering water and cook, stirring, until it thickens. Beat in the butter and lemon juice.
To serve, cut the warm pudding into squares and pour over the sauce. Leftovers may be served cold. Serves 4-6.

Raisin Pie

This popular Amish dessert, also known as Rosina Pie or Funeral Pie, uses a lattice top to cover a rich raisin sauce in a shortcrust pastry shell.

1 quantity shortcrust pastry (see Rhubarb Pie, page 68)

FILLING
1 cup raisins
2 cups water
1 cup sugar
4 Tbsps all-purpose flour
Pinch of salt
1 egg, well beaten
Juice and grated rind of 1 lemon

Prepare the pastry according to the Rhubarb Pie recipe, chill, then use half to line a greased 9-inch pie plate, reserving the trimmings. For the filling, soak the raisins in the water for 3 hours. Mix the sugar, flour, and salt together in a large heatproof bowl then carefully mix in the egg and lemon rind and juice. Add the raisins and liquid, stirring in well. Set the bowl over a pan of hot water and cook the raisin mixture for 15 minutes, stirring often. When the mixture has thickened, remove the bowl from the pan of water and leave to cool.
Preheat the oven to 450° F. When the mixture has cooled, pour into the prepared dough case. Roll out the remaining dough and cut into strips, place on the filling in a criss-cross fashion to form a lattice top, sealing the edges with a little water. Bake the pie in the oven for 10 minutes, then reduce the temperature to 350° F, and bake for another 25-30 minutes, or until the pie crust is brown. Serves 6.

Above: an Amish woman returning from a sale.

Rhubarb Pie

A spring and summer dish, rhubarb is served as a dessert or in salads. Pies are popular, as well as a crumble made with cinnamon and oatmeal which is sometimes served for birthday parties.

PASTRY
2 cups all-purpose flour
¼ cup butter or margarine
¼ cup shortening
About 4 Tbsps water

FILLING
4 cups diced, young rhubarb stalks
1-2 cups sugar, depending on taste
¼ cup all-purpose flour

To make the pastry, sift the flour with the salt into a mixing bowl. Cut in the butter and shortening until the mixture resembles coarse bread crumbs. Stir in enough water to form a dough. Wrap the dough and chill for 30 minutes.

Preheat the oven to 50° F. To make the filling, place the rhubarb in a large bowl. Mix the sugar and flour together then stir into the rhubarb until evenly coated. Leave to stand for 10-15 minutes. Roll half the dough out on a floured surface and use to line a greased 9-inch pie dish. Pile the rhubarb mixture into the dough case. Roll out the remaining dough to form a lid for the pie. Dampen the edge of the dough case and put on the lid. Press the edges firmly together to seal and trim if necessary. Cut two slits in the top of the pie to allow the steam to escape. Bake in the oven for 10 minutes, then reduce the heat to 350° F and bake for another 35-40 minutes, or until the crust is golden. Serves 6.

Dutch Pancake

Although known as Pennsylvania Dutch, this is actually a mispronunciation of deutsch, *and the German influence is clear in this baked pancake.*

Butter
½ cup all-purpose flour
Pinch of salt
3 eggs, beaten
½ cup milk
Powdered sugar
1 lemon, cut in wedges

Preheat the oven to 400° F. Grease a large, round cake pan. Sift the flour into a bowl along with the salt. Make a well in the center of the flour and add the eggs and milk. Beat with a wooden spoon, gradually mixing in the flour from the outside until a smooth batter is formed. Pour the batter into the pan. Place the pancake in the oven and bake for about 25 minutes until well risen and golden brown. Sprinkle with powdered sugar, and serve with lemon wedges to squeeze over the top.

Above: two Amish girls, dressed as their mothers and grandmothers before them. Right: the kitchen at the David Bradford House, Washington Pennsylvania.

Lemon Sponge Pie

A pie which can be prepared in advance and served cold is often the best choice when a large family gathering is planned.

1 quantity shortcrust pastry (see Cheesecake recipe opposite)

LEMON SPONGE FILLING
1 cup sugar
2 eggs, separated
Juice and grated rind of 1 lemon
1 Tbsp margarine, melted
3 Tbsps all-purpose flour
1 cup milk
Lemon slices to decorate
Powdered sugar
Whipped cream to serve (optional)

Prepare the pastry in the same way as for the Cheesecake recipe and use to line a greased 10-inch pie plate. Chill the pastry crust for 30 minutes before filling.
Preheat the oven to 350°F. Beat the sugar and egg yolks together until thick. Stir in the lemon juice, rind, margarine, and flour. Add the milk and mix well. Beat the egg whites until stiff peaks form, then fold into the lemon mixture. Pour into the chilled pastry crust and bake the pie for about 50 minutes, or until the filling is puffed and set and the pastry is golden. Allow to cool, then decorate with lemon slices and sprinkle with powdered sugar. The pie can be served with whipped cream, if desired. Serves 6.

Cheesecake

With almost every farm having its own dairy, where much of the work is done by the women, fresh cheese is bound to feature in the dessert menu.

½ cup shortening
1½ cups all-purpose flour
¼ tsp salt
Ice water
1 pound cream cheese
4 eggs, beaten
1 cup sugar
2 Tbsps all-purpose flour
1 cup cream
1 tsp vanilla extract
Cinnamon

Rub the shortening into the flour and salt until the mixture resembles bread crumbs. Work in enough ice

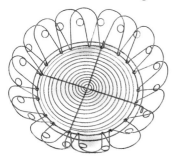

water to make a firm dough. Roll out on a floured surface and use to line the bottom and sides of a 10-inch springform pan.
Preheat the oven to 400°F. Place a sheet of baking paper over the pastry and cover it with dry rice or beans. Bake the pastry for about 10 minutes until just starting to brown lightly. Remove the paper and rice or beans and return the pastry to the oven for 5 minutes to bake the bottom.
Beat the cream cheese to soften, then gradually beat in the eggs. Beat in the sugar and flour. Stir in the cream gradually and add the vanilla extract. Pour into the pastry shell and place in the oven. Lower the temperature to 325°F and bake for 40 minutes. Sprinkle with cinnamon and cool completely before serving. Serves 6.

Apple Strudel

It takes practice to get the strudel pastry as thin as it should be for this recipe, an art which Amish girls learn by watching their mothers. With fresh apples from the family orchard, apple and fruit desserts are popular with the Amish.

2 Tbsps shortening
2½ cups all-purpose flour
1 tsp salt
2 eggs, beaten
½ cup warm water
½ cup butter, melted
4 cups peeled, sliced apples
Grated rind and juice of 1 lemon
1 cup brown sugar
½ cup golden raisins
½ cup chopped walnuts
½ cup fine bread crumbs
½ tsp cinnamon
Ice cream or whipped cream to serve

Rub the shortening into the flour and salt until the mixture resembles bread crumbs. Mix in the eggs and enough water to make a soft, but not sticky, dough. Knead the dough, then throw or beat it against a clean table top until it is smooth and elastic and stretches easily without tearing. Cover the dough and leave to rest for 30 minutes.

Combine all the remaining ingredients, except the melted butter, in a bowl. Mix together well and spoon in 3 Tbsps of the butter. Reserve the rest of the butter for the pastry. Preheat the oven to 400° F. Cover the table with a large clean cloth such as a tablecloth or a pastry cloth, lightly flour it then roll out the dough to a 15-inch square. Using floured fingertips, pull the dough from the middle, out to the ends, lifting it each time, until it is as thin as paper. Sprinkle the reserved butter over the pastry. Quickly scatter the filling mixture evenly over the pastry. Fold in the outer edges and lift one end of the cloth to help roll the pastry over the filling to form a long roll about 4 inches thick.

Place the strudel on a baking sheet; if it won't fit in a straight line, form it into a crescent shape. Bake for about 20-30 minutes, or until golden brown and flaky. Allow to cool until barely warm, then sprinkle with powdered sugar. Cut into serving pieces and serve with ice cream or whipped cream. Serves 4-6.

Above: the Paradise Mennonite Church, in Paradise, Pennsylvania. Right: a young Amish woman selling produce at the local farmer's market.

72

Streusel Bread

Amish children learn their cooking skills by helping out in the kitchen and watching their mothers. They would rarely be taught difficult techniques – there is little time for that – but would learn through observing.

½ cup butter
¾ cup sugar
1 package active dry yeast
¼ cup lukewarm water
1 cup milk
2 eggs, beaten
2½-3 cups bread flour

TOPPING
1¼ cups soft bread crumbs
1 tsp cinnamon
3 Tbsps brown sugar
2 Tbsps butter, melted

Cream the butter and sugar together in a large bowl. Dissolve the yeast in the lukewarm water and leave until frothy, about 5-10 minutes.

Scald the milk and gradually add to the butter and sugar. When slightly cooled, add the eggs and the yeast mixture. Mix well, then work in the flour to make a thick batter. Add more flour if the batter is too runny. Beat the mixture with a spatula or wooden spoon; it will be too soft to knead by hand. Cover the bowl and leave the batter in a cool place for about 1 hour to rise until doubled in bulk.

Grease two deep pie dishes, large loaf pans or brioche pans and spoon in the batter to fill just over halfway. Mix together the topping ingredients and sprinkle over the top of each bread. Leave in a warm place for about 20 minutes to rise again. Preheat the oven to 400°F. Bake the loaves for about 20 minutes, or until golden brown. Serve with butter or jam. Makes 2 loaves.

Corn Bread

This is a sweet cake-style corn bread which can be served with cheese.

1 cup yellow cornmeal
1 cup all-purpose flour
4 Tbsps sugar
1 tsp salt
4 Tsps baking powder
1 egg, beaten
1 cup milk
2 Tbsps shortening, melted

Grease an 8-inch square baking pan and preheat the oven to 400°F. Mix the cornmeal, flour, sugar, salt, and baking powder in a large bowl. Make a well in the center and add the egg, milk, and melted shortening. Beat very well until the ingredients are thoroughly blended. Pour the batter into the prepared pan and bake until risen and golden brown on top. As a variation, add ¼ cup of grated sharp cheese. Cut into squares to serve. Serves 4-6.

Above: a preschooler playing in the family buggy. Right: hard at work in the fields.

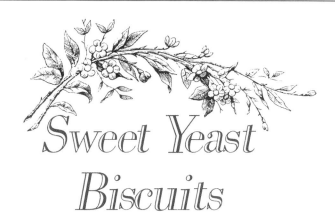

Sweet Yeast Biscuits

Not traditional cookies, these are risen yeast cakes made with a sweet dough. Famed for their baking skills, the Amish produce a bewildering array of baked goods from traditional breads to "make do" recipes which utilize whatever the cook has at hand.

4 cups milk
4 eggs, beaten
4 Tbsps butter, melted
1 package active dry yeast
½ cup lukewarm water
2 cups sugar
Flour

TOPPING
2 cups sugar
4 Tbsps all-purpose flour
½ cup butter, softened
4 Tbsps boiling water

Scald the milk and allow to cool slightly. Beat in the eggs gradually, along with the butter. Cool to lukewarm. Mix the yeast and water and add to the milk mixture with the sugar and enough flour to make a thin batter. Cover and leave in a warm place overnight.
Add enough flour to the mixture to make a soft, pliable dough. Knead it lightly on a well-floured surface. Place in a greased bowl and leave to rise again for about an hour until doubled in size.
Punch down the dough and knead again lightly. Roll out until 1-inch thick and cut out cookie shapes. Place on a greased baking sheet and leave to rise again until doubled in size, about 20 minutes.
Preheat the oven to 400°F. Mix the topping ingredients to a smooth paste and brush over the tops of the biscuits. Bake the biscuits for about 20 minutes, or until the bottoms sound hollow when tapped. Makes 1 dozen biscuits.

Molasses Doughnuts

For a social occasion, such as a fireworks celebration, Amish families enjoy standing over a hot fire to make delicious doughnuts – with molasses, naturally.

¾ pint milk
4 cups all-purpose flour
½ package of yeast
1½ Tbsps molasses
¼ cup butter
1 egg
Oil for deep-frying
Sugar

Scald the milk then leave until lukewarm. Stir in half the flour to make a smooth batter. Dissolve the yeast in a little warm water and add to the batter. Cover and leave to stand for at least 8 hours.
Cream the molasses, butter, and egg together with a little of the remaining flour. Add to the first mixture. Knead in enough of the remaining flour to make a light dough that can be rolled out. Place in a large greased bowl and cover with a floured cloth. Leave in a warm place to rise for about an hour until doubled in bulk.

Roll out on a floured board and cut into doughnut rings. Leave to rise again for about 20 minutes. Heat the oil in a deep-fryer or pan to about 375°F. Add the doughnuts a few at a time and fry until they rise to the surface and puff up. When they are cooked through, drain them on paper towels. Roll in sugar while still warm, if desired. Makes about 12 doughnuts.

Walnut Raisin Cookies

At Christmas, it is traditional to prepare ten kinds of cookies; nuts, fruit, and cinnamon are the most popular ingredients used.

1 cup butter
1½ cups light brown sugar
3 eggs
1 tsp baking soda dissolved in 1½ Tbsps hot water
3¼ cups all-purpose flour
½ tsp salt
1 tsp cinnamon
1 cup walnuts, chopped
1 cup golden raisins

Preheat the oven to 350°F. Cream the butter and sugar together until light. Beat in the eggs, one at a time. Add the soda mixture, then work in half the flour, together with the salt and cinnamon. Mix in the walnuts and raisins, then the remaining flour. Grease several baking sheets and drop the mixture by spoonfuls about 1 inch apart. Bake for about 8-10 minutes, or until golden brown. Makes 3 dozen cookies.

Sand Tarts

Called sand tarts because of the grainy mixture of sugar and nuts on the top, these cookies would be one of the first types of recipe mastered by the girls of the household and cooked for guests and family.

1¼ cups granulated sugar
1 cup butter
1 egg, beaten
2 cups all-purpose flour
1 egg white, lightly beaten
Sugar
Finely chopped pecans or walnuts

Cream the sugar and butter together until light. Beat in the egg and gradually add the flour, working it in well to make a stiff dough. It may not be necessary to use all the flour. Chill the mixture overnight, or until firm enough to roll out.

Preheat the oven to 350°F. Flour a board or pastrycloth well and roll out the dough in small portions. Cut into 2- or 3-inch circles with a cookie cutter.
Place on greased baking sheets. Brush the tops with beaten egg white and sprinkle with a mixture of sugar and nuts. Bake for about 10 minutes, or until crisp and pale golden. Leave a few minutes on the baking sheets then remove to wire cooling racks. Makes 3 dozen tarts.

Above: a group of Amish women at a barn raising pausing for refreshment.

Index

ACKNOWLEDGEMENTS

The publishers would like to thank home economist Sue Philpot and
stylist Blake Minton for their contribution to the photographs on
pages 2-3, 12-13, 20-21, 28-29, 48-49, 62-63, and the front cover.